AUTOBIOGRAPHY
OF A
WOUND

PITT POETRY SERIES
ED OCHESTER, EDITOR

AUTOBIOGRAPHY

OF A

WOUND

BRYNNE REBELE-HENRY

UNIVERSITY OF PITTSBURGH PRESS

This book is the winner of the 2017 Donald Hall Prize for Poetry, awarded by the Association of Writers and Writing Programs (AWP). AWP, a national organization serving more than three hundred colleges and universities, has its headquarters at George Mason University, Mail Stop 1E3, Fairfax, VA 22030.

The Donald Hall Prize for Poetry is made possible by the generous support of Amazon.com.

Published by the University of Pittsburgh Press, Pittsburgh, Pa., 15260
Copyright © 2018, Brynne Rebele-Henry
Manufactured in the United States of America
Printed on acid-free paper
10 9 8 7 6 5 4 3 2 1

ISBN 13: 978-0-8229-6567-1

Cover art by Karen Constance
Cover design by Melissa Dias-Mandoly

CONTENTS

Scarab with device of kneeling fertility figure before obelisk   3

Portrait of a female figure with puncture marks & frayed rope   4

Self-portrait as a woman with a bullet wound   6

Self-portrait as a girl made out of stone   7

Self-portrait as a broken Venus statuette   8

Definition of Girl   11

Definition of a Fist   12

Definition of Basalt   13

Definition of Bleeding   14

Definition of a Broken Wrist   15

Aubade for a dying girl   16

Aubade for a wound   21

Aubade for a marble child   22

Self-portrait with needles & a broken mouth   23

Self-portrait as a wound   24

Female fertility figure, bone, carved, B.C.   27

Portrait as yourself   29

Portrait as a menstruating figure   30

Portrait as a dying man   31

Portrait as a bleeding woman   32

Self-portrait as the boys who died & the girls who were turned to bones   33

Picture of F, myself & a lake town   34

Picture of three girls, a white house & F   35

Picture of the lost children & the first menstruation   36

Self-portrait as the lake in which they were drowned   37

Self-portrait as a girl without a body   38

Self-portrait as a fertility figure   39

Self-portrait as a drowning city   40

Figure of Isis/Aphrodite   41

Self-portrait as split-open lips, a gun & a cornfield at night   42

Self-portrait as a wound, a bird skull & a stone   45

The brief life of a marble woman   46

The brief life of a wound   47

The brief life of a girl   48

The brief life of a stone figure   49

The death of S, Aphrodite & the kneeling basilisk   50

The carving of S/Aphrodite & F   51

Marble female figure   52

The pathos of fertility, 1921, Germany   53

Standing female figure wearing a strap & a necklace   54

Figure of fertility goddess (2700 B.C.)   55

Figure of fertility goddess (2000 B.C.)   56

Plaque with nude female in a shrine niche   57

Terracotta statuette of a nude woman   58

Head of a woman, 220 B.C.   59

Kneeling female deity   61

The history of bones   62

The history of violence   63

Self-biography as a hole   64

Self-biography as a Venus   65

Self-biography as a false saint   66

Self-biography as a pregnant woman   67

Self-biography as a girl with no mouth   68

Autobiography of a Venus figure   69

Autobiography of something fertile   70

Autobiography of basalt & broken stones   71

Autobiography of a wound   72

Notes and Acknowledgments   73

AUTOBIOGRAPHY
OF A
WOUND

Scarab with device of kneeling fertility figure before obelisk

The figure is carved from glazed steatite and the woman is kneeling,
stomach bulging so wide it's unholy, in front of an obelisk. Her knees
look worn down and knobby, and she wears a bent paper crown

Once I went feral, broke myself inside of myself
so all that was left was shards. At night I'd pray
to small faceless stones I'd collected, worry them until my fingers
carved them small with age and turned them wizened,
splitting at their seams. When I stopped praying I started eating
then I stopped eating and that was better than praying,
I started eating again and then stopped saying no
so I was always on my knees
hunched underneath some girl's shuddering hand,
salt filling the spaces under my tongue
like a baptism, like something pure,
like something a girl can call clean

Whenever I want to cry
I make myself laugh, so my laughter always sounds like the ragged inhale
before screaming

I might be a slut but I don't spend much time in bed, prefer the ground
or underneath a bed, on the floor of that girl's attic, dust gathering
in the folds of my skin, pressing into my mouth like a communion wafer.
All I need to be pretty is salt and old bruises

I let them grind my body down until all that's left is bone,
small and sore underneath. Beauty is destruction so
she calls me a broken animal, a shard of glass, a child
before a barrel is placed against her head, a mouth
worn down until it is nothing

Portrait of a female figure with puncture marks & frayed rope

Because a man is taught that his anger is A: a god
B: a burning house, a burning church, a girl with a phone cord
wrapped around her neck, broken capillaries like swarmed fish

Dear man:

Once I would call a kiss a bruise because they all bruised me with them,
girls biting into me until I was nothing, until my veins shifted under their teeth,
until the breath knocked out of me and I sat there dumb and dead at 15

The victim was wearing a wedding dress, a house coat, purple cotton underwear,
her lips were shell pink but by the time he was done they were the blue of
burning cities, lapis lazuli, oxygen deficiency pigmenting her mouth like an old-
time Hollywood girl's eyelids, always flickering like electric lights

Her hands were:
1. On her chest
2. Held up as if in prayer, as if begging, palms making a small temple
3. Splayed out behind her

The evidence points to: a stranger, a serial, a small man
who everyone says
is gentle
A man everyone believes

That she must have pushed him over the edge somehow,
with her girlness
or with her smallness

A girl is something to be consumed, a girl is prey, a small flickering light
held in an open throat

The violations: handing me a bottle and whispering *drink*
*until you can't speak/get on your hands & knees for me/*waking up to a body not my
own/waking up unto blood

I learned early that beauty is violence so I always opened myself up to it.
In bed I'd tell her to use her fist even when we both knew I couldn't take it.
When I wear lipstick I match it to the same dirty shade of my first blood.

When I cry it is only for others' benefit.
Everyone likes to see a pretty girl with her face crumpled
into a hurt beyond recognition or, better yet,
dead somewhere with her legs open.

Self-portrait as a woman with a bullet wound

capillaries like small fish
because men are taught that their fear is a god we are all dying
by the time I turned thirteen I learned how to hide from the men who had
started following me like blood insects through streets/how to still yourself when
men
brush up against you and whisper *bitch*
once a girl asked *but what would you let me do*
and I said *everything but a loaded gun*

sometimes, I dream that I know the taste of bullets
like flint, river stones
I used to cover my body with jasmine oil to hide the stench of
menstruation/like iron and death on my skin
once I learned what it means to have hands around your neck
but I already knew what it's like to be almost dead, already knew to open
my mouth to swallow the bullet, how to become nothing but an exit hole

Self-portrait as a girl made out of stone

Dear F

When I got beautiful I got endangered and then I had to learn how to stop my mouth from quivering/how to swallow fear like a handful of blue pills/how to still my hips when I walked/I learned how to eat cake batter straight up/how to chew mint leaves until my teeth turn green/I learned how to spit at the earth until it spat back/I started keeping mace and makeshift knives in my pockets/I colored my mouth the same color as the worms and pretended to be nothing but stone.

Self-portrait as a broken Venus statuette

Cherry blossom wound: my stomach was torn open, the flesh petal-like, the scar
a blood-mouth, ribcage going staccato like messy buildings. They said the first
woman was a small crimson being with no teeth named Blood.

Once a girl I knew kept her teeth in a small gold box, like sticky pearls.
Oh B, don't you know that flowers are really small suicides and that every body is
a blood myth? At thirteen I'd butterfly a knife between my fingers to see if I'd
bleed. I learned the hidden meanings of flowers: they're all wounds.

Once a girl sent me funeral lilies every day for months. That year I studied blue
things, painted my lips redder than the blood of my insides.

Once a girl's mother tried to call for her but all that came out of her mouth was
rain. The bodies of queer girls are never safe. Our flesh turned into politics,
statements in the form of broken ribs, a baseball bat to the skull.

What do you call it when girls keep dying, what do you call it when your body is
a zeppelin? How do you become something other than wounds?
At six months old they sliced my stomach open like a gourd: even now it still feels
hollow. When I put my hand to my womb: nothing but air & blood & the scar
like a fishing hook, knotted flesh.

The scar from the scalpel is five inches long. I can still feel the metal gutting me. I
can still feel the tenuousness of my insides.

Slowly, at fourteen, I forgot my scars.
Slowly, I became someone.

Dear F

What do you do when you're bleeding again at fifteen/when you take pills and
get shots but can't stop the blood/when everything you own is stained? What do
you do when your body becomes a wound? What do you do when your scars
open back up again? When one day you put your hand to your mouth and find
nothing?

Dear F

My stomach is held together by a thread: a scar the width of fishing wire, like a knot under my skin. Sometimes, I think it will open again like a gutted fish: the red pearls of my ovaries spilling out like burst seeds. Sometimes, I can already feel myself dying. Sometimes I wish for something to pray to.

Dear F

If I had to love something it would be the color red. If I could I would wear only crimson, I would become a girl more blood than not. I would paint my lips like a dying city. I would be as beautiful as blood and honey.

Dear F

I miss A. At the blue house I looked at marble statuettes. I found you in the Georgia heat. Your pumice body worn down from prayer, stomach and cunt rendered with brushstrokes. At the museum I think about giving you a shrine, shovel sour fruit candy into my mouth/I wish to become something fertile like you, both animal and not.

Dear F

I don't like children and I can't give birth. When I bleed it is futile red. One day, I think my womb will collapse, turn to nothing but dust. One day, I think I will be both human and not. Once, I swallowed someone else's blood. Once, I was afraid of death and would wash my hands until they welted and the skin scraped off. I know so much about blood I can sense it before it is spilled, can feel the wounds before they are made.

Dear F

My nails are always painted the color of blood clots. I wear stilettos every day. I want to become something more vampire than not. I want to have a body made out of crimson stone. If I could be a color let it be red.

Dear F

A girl I knew broke her arm so many times the bones became only dirt. Once, I saw some boys crush the bodies of tadpoles with river stones. At eight I filled my pockets with sand and rocks and thought I could become something less human. Now I'm always wearing leather. Now I'm always looking to decipher the moon's cycle and rimming my eyes with liner and burning sage like I could be purified.

Dear F

One day we will both turn to dust, the pale sugar we ate mixed with red juice will stain our teeth, soreness still crammed between our gums. We will be beautiful and deadly. They will remember us for our bones and how our blood always tasted like honey.

Definition of Girl

the scars, every time my grandmother clicked her teeth,
said a girl isn't a girl when she gets fat/everyone watch the pig eat,
eat dirt because it has no calories/ride a horse down a ravine in a
thunderstorm and let the branches cut your face/I never swim
because I'm afraid of blood and drowning/but I always break
my own bones anyway

Definition of a Fist

A girl saying *close your eyes/open your mouth*/a girl saying *slut/let me bruise these thighs*/two bottles of wine and an attic/a girl whispering *someday someone else will love you when I don't*/broken bed/bleeding out and on the floor thinking your ribcage is made of imploding stars/remembering that we are all dying

Definition of Basalt

A girl broken into stone/if you could pray would you/pig's guts and honey/a half-lit Marlboro used as a prayer candle/saying *please/don't leave me empty*/opening your mouth and begging for a storm

Definition of Bleeding

One day I will open my mouth but all that will come out is red

Definition of a Broken Wrist

I am still learning how to be hurt, how to let the floorboards cut into my back. One day I will open my legs and all that will come out is dust and birds. One day my lips will be gold leaf. One day I will no longer have eyes.

Aubade for a dying girl

1.

F says,
Sometimes I miss being anorexic-inclined.
It's so much easier when everyone can see your creation:
the way you carved yourself a new body,
turned your skeleton into the outside of you. It's much easier
to not eat than it is to eat, every thought replaced by a dumb buzz,
by a hand pressing your collapsing ribcage until it hurts. Getting
on the scale and listening to the nurses call you a tiny thing,
nothing but air, like you could slip out of your body and its danger.
But I could never commit to it,
only stopped eating a few days at a time then binged on grease
but didn't do anything to expel it, just ate until there were stones
in my stomach and silk felt tight on my neck.
Everyone wants to fuck a dying girl. Everyone wants to fuck
a girl whose skeleton has swallowed her: a prelude to her death,
a building's structure without the fear of collapse, a war
burning inside her body like filthy suns.

2.

My first memory is of the dark. Burning in my stomach, the tube
swallowed me and then peeled back my flesh until they could see inside it,
into something both my body and not.

3.

At thirteen we'd all flirt with death. Spend hours absorbed in our veins, or
watching her slice little parts of her fingers open, then, later, small parts of
her wrists. I learned how to take my clothes off without shaking hands,
how to swallow vodka so it burns, how to claw the insides of my thighs
underneath the table. At night, as the train passes through and shakes her
house, we watch the scars glisten on our half-naked bodies. When two dead
girls love each other, it's a funeral, the kind you can't resurrect, where no
one grows wings of fire or gets drunk in the back of a truck, where you
bring razors and ointment to anoint each other with.

4.

I mix liquors and stumble around the city, don't recognize my reflection
in mirrors. I always try to scald the afterfeel of someone else's spit drying
in my mouth and the back of my neck, the way a girl says *But I won't
stay/I'm not really/gay/like you/don't hold my hand/in public/why can't you be
a boy?*

5.

I never say no so I always have some girl's lipstick in my teeth. We teach
each other how to love someone else for more than a night, how to
swallow a girl's silt-cum until our throats close up with it. I go to her
church with cum in my hair and we drink vodka and I let her cut into the
insides of me with her fingers. She says it feels like she's fucking an
angel/like I'm a girl resurrected/like I'm already dead and nobody even
had to kill me.

Aubade for a wound

Tell me it wasn't red,
that when we bled it was only
cobwebs in the shape of a broken womb,
that the stitches were eyelashes twitching open,
the shadow of a girl at night and a flickering lamp
in a verde room filled with someone else's dead,
ghosts lining the insides of my mouth like fillings, gold
flashing out through my insides, rubbing stones until
they wore to dust and praying to something larger
than ourselves, watching the bones shift until
I was no longer safe, until I was something to be hunted,
scarred myself so no one else could do it for me,
a girl isn't a woman until she's been broken
so I broke myself until my body was only dust
and someone else's hands, until my veins turned
so barren they couldn't get needles in,
something more refuse than girl.

Aubade for a marble child

You will suck in your stomach and in doing so absolve the bulge of your flesh. You will grind your teeth until the metal cuts the inside of your mouth. You will dream of being a girl's body turned to air. You will cut little lines into yourself at twelve. You will write on your body with nails, make carvings on yourself at eight and call it practice, but not know what you're practicing for. You will develop a fear of needles, and even now you can't hold a certain type of knife without shaking. You will swear to never have a child but at night you will dream of them, small and blood-wet and carved from marble. You will always be another girl's shame, a smoked-up half-secret whispered only when high, teeth marks you can't conceal, a girl's bed surrounded by flickering candles and small vodka bottles at 3 a.m., sun rising onto your splayed bodies, onto her messy lips. And she'll dip apples in ocean water and say bless you/bless us/bless this and rub her citron hands over yours until you're both blessed by something other than yourselves, snow catching in your hair and knotting itself there. You will always have that hollow from years ago: a burning thicket, a bone-deep cut, a small mountain turning your body to both stone and something bloodier.

Self-portrait with needles & a broken mouth

"let me break you, turn you to a girl gone red and open"

One day, we will again be loved, I will again open my mouth
and let a girl place her fingers inside, gunmetalsweat.
One day, we will again promise, we will drink tap water
mixed with salt in an effort to clean out our throats,
we will no longer chart our ribs with a marker,
we will no longer shake from the sight of stars.
At night, we will comb each other's hair and get drunk on nothing,
and one day, we will open our eyes, we will again love,
our bodies will never again be broken and we will
step into the dawn with nothing in our hands, we will
let our scars turn into small birds.

Self-portrait as a wound

My wrists scraped raw abrasions small poppies,
girls' bodies are always seen as fields
something to be maimed, something to be plowed,
so I let my body be landscaped into something not mine

A girl is:
1. something to be filled, an orifice or other form of hole
2. something to be claimed
3. dead

Dear F

I never say no. I learned how to say yes at fourteen. I want a body made
of stone: both penetrable and not.

The closest thing to a girl is a hole:
something to be filled/something to be broken

after I fucked her, she said the prettiest thing
a girl can be is sad

the second best thing to being sad is being anorexic
so we stop eating, let our bones overtake the rest of us,
turn us spinal and empty, into girls whose bodies could be cathedrals:
something both holy and not

Autopsy of the wound:

(sum of the wound)

Dreams of your body covered in bruises/wants to break your body
open/talks about your smallness, how your bones feel crushable/will say
this is not yours and you'll nod. After, she'll usually say *it's mine/only I can
make you bleed*/wants your body to be broken down

Causation of the wound:

a broken planet, three spackle scars, a girl and a barely lit candle at night

Female fertility figure, bone, carved, B.C.

*"The female figure has a carved head, ears and nose, with incised lines to
indicate her mouth and eyes, and other lines at her neck, belly, and pelvis.
Breasts, buttocks, legs, and feet are carved in three dimensions, and there are
small holes where arms might have been attached."*

I wanted to know the limits of what a girl's body could hold
so I told her to do anything she wanted.
Later in a strange girl's attic I'll assist in my own destruction.
My grandmother said skinny is the closest you can get
to being something more than a girl so I stopped eating.
At night, I'd finger the ridges growing between my bones
like gothic architecture, and I'd cry, wouldn't stop until I could hear
my bones click like rosaries, hipbones a stretch of mean,
a belly so sharp no girl could lie on top of me without bruises after, mutual
penance. Then I went back to brushing my hair until it fell out,
rubbing flavored lipgloss on my mouth and waiting
for spring like it could save me.

I learned that getting on my knees
was the closest I could get to a holy act, so now
I'm always kneeling down for someone.

Dear F

I learned about the magic of bleeding the time I fell down and skinned a bulb of flesh out of myself. Still have small woundmarks etched into my body. A hand-length slash on my belly, small nubby silvers on my wrists and breasts, a crescent on my collarbone, a bitemark on my inner thigh that never healed, spackle marks on my legs and feet, patches on my knees. A few years later I'll be wearing white silk pants and find them soaked red: salvation, and not. Wild animals will chew their limbs off when trapped, but I settled for drawing sewing needles through the pads of my fingers, writing letters on the insides of my legs with bruises.

Portrait as yourself

As a child your brain fires random synapses and you almost die several times. You don't sleep because you think you will die again, your heart is a broken animal. Years later you will be sad and then not. You will draw flowers on your skin. You will become something.

Portrait of a menstruating figure

Gemstones against my thighs

I wanted nothing more than to be saved
I wanted nothing more than to never bleed again
I cried as the blood coursed down my leg
I wanted to be nothing but bleach

Dear F

I'm bleeding as I write this. My skin gives
off the sick copper scent of iron like old coins
and menstruation. I have red on my clothes.
I never wear white. Whenever I menstruate
I almost vomit from the pain, bleed so much that I get anemic.
Faint when I try to eat meat and go nauseated from the blood clots
like dead things like giving birth to wounds.
Find blood spatters like small murders on my clothes.

Once I had a shot to stop the bleeding but it wore away the insides of my womb
and I bled every day for months.

The first time a girl made me bleed was on a mattress on the floor and afterward
she called me an angel.

Dear B

You will wear something red every day for luck. You will discover how to chart
constellations. Your hair will turn obsidian. Your body will no longer be a
wounded thing.

Portrait as a dying man

Dear Lord: ribcages are meant to be broken.
For a few days I ate only apples.
For a few months I tried to be something not-girl,
hid my breasts and wore loose clothing.

If a straight man dies it's a tragedy/if a woman dies it's expected/a warning for
other women/*don't go running by yourself/don't wear tight clothes/don't drink from open
glasses.*

If I could I would swallow my own rib and create some new creature. I would
have a body composed of nothing but dry petals and thorns.

Portrait as a bleeding woman

Female blood is drawn like a well.
That's why they made F and the others from marble and pumice.
You can't draw blood from a stone.
You can't break a fleshless girl.
I want to be built like a rock
so it's impossible to wound me
without skinning the flesh off your own hands in the process.
I want to be milk from the earth.
Once a girl I knew put pebbles in her ears and they lodged there.
Once a girl I knew huffed nail polish
and kept marbles and cigarette butts
from her mother's club in her pockets.
Once I ran out of blood I decided to become stone.

Self-portrait as the boys who died & the girls who were turned to bones

We will light candles for their bodies and sing to the flames.
We will say *Orlando*, we will say *Bullet*.
The week before, I was torn open.
Once I woke up to a body no longer my own.

Picture of F, myself & a lake town

We eat sticks of butter in Michigan.
I can take a fist like it's breathing.
Scar tissue.
F says, *swallow the stones and the asphalt,*
become something stone. Become something. Eat rocks.
It's easier to be impenetrable so I swallow handfuls
of pebbles then eat cunt.
They said my name was Hoover,
said only ugly girls eat like pigs/said your thighs should be bones,
fuckability is how close to death your body is.
But I'm always taking my clothes off.
At the lake we eat sand, we eat dirt and little shards of granite.
F says, *the best thing a girl can be is indestructible/the best thing a girl can be is*
unfuckable so I let her turn my body into basalt.

Picture of three girls, a white house & F

She says, *I want to snort coke off your ass/I want to use your body like a paper cup.*
When F and I go to the white house we drink only whole milk, wear nothing but
our spit. It's winter and our nakedness is like snow. We eat icicles. I tell F about
bleeding out on a mattress with a scarf tied around my wrists, the girl who
renamed me Slut. F sucks off the cream and we cut our palms with a kitchen
knife and swear blood sisters. After, F tells me her first name was Cunt, that she
was born unto bones and dirt. When I was a girl I always had soil in my teeth.
Now I'm almost pure. One night F turns around and says, *we could have been saints.*
In the dim light her stone cunt is a small continent. F says, *girls like us always have
cum under our nails and our asses up in the backs of cars, always have blood between
our teeth.* Then she shows me her first knife scar: a crooked ribbon. Says, *we're all
bitch gods.*

Picture of the lost children & the first menstruation

At eleven J bleeds onto the playground dirt
J says, *my body turned before I could*
We pray to our calluses
We eat the earth/we eat each other
We walk into streams looking for broken bottles
We drink pale juice and declare ourselves drunks
Her mother's arm broke open one morning, now all that's left is plastic

A girl says, *I know what it's like to be backhanded, I know what it's like to have broken more bones than not. The girl says, I know more about violence than I do about my own body.* It's summer and she and I collect minnows in buckets and watch them drown, we eat mud like it's communion and she prays to something larger than herself.

Self-portrait as the lake in which they were drowned

I wanted to be a girl gone stone so I got naked in the water.
One day I looked down and found blood.
We drank ocean water mixed with vodka,
the sky a broken reckoning.
When I walked through the snow I found my body.
I will be stone. I will be fertile.
In my dreams I'm always drowning, in my dreams her hands are small birds.
Once we ate snow mixed with syrup and got sick off ice.
I held a molar in my palm.
In the fall we didn't eat and drank kahlua,
had sex in churches. Once I waded into an ocean, salt and chlorine.
Once a girl said she could teach me how to drown.
Forgive me for I have learned the feeling of hands wrapped
around my neck, for I have learned how to break,
for in the summer I became something other than pure stone,
for I have swallowed blood, both my own and not.

Self-portrait as a girl without a body

Once I knew a girl named Blue, at night I'd dream
about her toothlessness, how when she opened her mouth
there was nothing but lake and dark.
Once I was gutted like a fish on Sunday, my scar
a seam undoing. Every night I lit candles for the girls
named after their blood and prayed for a year free of bones.

Self-portrait as a fertility figure

At thirteen we wrapped tape measures around our thighs,
learned how to suck until our flesh was hollowed,
how to etch little lines with a Sharpie into our fat.
At night we'd stain our lips the red of our hymens and get naked on couches.
One of the girls called me Slut because I was like a hole of a girl:
always consuming something/always swallowing.
When I was a model I'd rim my mouth with lip gloss so it looked like cunt.
When we were girls we learned how to swish our hips and detach our jaws.
One of the girls gets gay off cosmos. Another slashes lines into herself
and begs for summer. One girl says, *your new name is Hole/your new name is Whore.*
That summer I started wearing sequins like scabs,
started kissing strange girls in bathrooms and casting bones.

Self-portrait as a drowning city

When we walked into the water, it was only
so we could drown, salt flush-throated,
hands to the air, tried to baptize the twisted
girlness out of us, but instead we just swallowed
chlorine until we got sick from it.
Once, I loved a girl who was a burning thicket.
Once, I tried to be pure.
Forgive me, for I have been split open,
for I have let my body turn to something
other than stone, for I have been in love
but have also lost. I tell her I would purge,
I would use my rib for a necklace.
We spit watermelon seeds into the water
like little organs. I crush grapes with my molars
and grind until everything splits open and the juice runs.
I say make my body a building/and light it on fire.
We walk home, your wings stuck to your back
with Elmer's glue, feathers between my teeth
and the glitter we doused ourselves in, gasoline
to try to again be pure, to become a million small planets.

Figure of Isis/Aphrodite

I got fucked up in the mountains
my throat felt like afterbirth
the hotel's closet
thighs/bruise/thrash/your hands/too-long nails
then we took our clothes off and the water was spit-like
I thought the pennies could be barnacles against my knees
I'm not very good at bending down
once, I wanted to be someone
but then I decided to waste my life
I'm sorry
your skin was chlorine, vodka-tongue
once, you bought a butterfly knife
it made a spreadsheet on your thighs
I like to imagine my own death
soon I will pull out my teeth and will
you say my name?
sometimes I get sick off sex
let girls etch into my thighs
with their too-sharp teeth
once, I tried to be somebody
once, we both tried to be good
but then decided to become gods
something always burning
something both dead and not

Self-portrait as split-open lips, a gun & a cornfield at night

Girl (a definition):
a broken bone, the scars she left
on my thigh, three empty bottles
of vodka, a rib cage twisted
inside of itself, your hand covered in red
from when you broke open the inside of me

*

Her lipstick smeared like drying wounds
on my thighs & so I didn't know
that I too was bleeding & that my blood
could make me holy, so that night
I washed the fingers of the girls
off of me, started clean & the next morning
we drank until our organs felt transparent—
I regretted it, but I always regret it
that sharp after-shame, bruises
like a penance, that's what I call them

                *

Once I kissed a girl and she told me
to call her a god so I did

                *

Men tell me they'll kill me, that
I'm a girl gone air, but a girl's body
is a grave & so my legs must
become open caskets

*

What do you call a dying girl?
A: a new god, a burning gun, a small pair of hands

Self-portrait as a wound, a bird skull & a stone

(speaking as S and Aphrodite as seventeen-year-old girls)

The cats still in the dark outside your house,
at the beach we let the sand chap our bodies
into something not our bodies and you drew
lines over my skin with the crooked edges of shells
and we forgot your fingers on my spine in the night.
Your father is a man turned to stone,
one of these days we will find him rocked over
on the very same porch step but this time
his eyes won't open again, or they will be open
and unblinking, shards of broken-bottle blue
and a half-whispered promise, the touch we tried to forget.
Your mother said a body is an engine
and girls like us are scorched, gasoline cans
left on the pavement. After the brushfire
we sat in your attic, sucked
the singe off our fingers, mouths full of soot.
Your father said to pray for a flood
so we started burning everything up,
let our knees start to blacken
and took up smoking, as if a lungfull
of ash could save us, as if the sky weren't red,
but some nights we still climb the reservoir,
swim until we can't anymore and then we float.

The brief life of a marble woman

We spend all our time in cars
F says let's chew cud and gum F says
let's eat stale fruit F drives into the city with
her stone belly painted blue and we walk
into a mall fountain and she says she wants to know
what happened to the others I say it doesn't matter
and I fill my pockets with fountain pennies and remember the time
I ate dirt and how it tasted like honey and oranges

The brief life of a wound

Dear F & A, I want to tell you about blood

As a kid I ate marker I drew on my body with nails we learned how to sing
we learned how to take a hit we became girls in the winter we learned how
to line our eyes with charcoal we became something feral we became less.

We drink the wine/I suck fingers/I open my mouth so my throat is a ready hole
/blood spackle on my thighs like cheap paint/blue-red pain/my vision blurs/I
still my breath/I think this is being dead/I close my eyes/I fall down/crawl on
the floor with my lips bared/I bleed so much her hands come away red/I bit my
lip/when I looked down it was blood/later I'll think about how once my body
was marble. How this is the life of a girl. I ate a bowl of fish eggs then drank wine
mixed with blood and honey, prayed to all the other dead things.

The brief life of a girl

When my mouth was a wound I was always fucking when I wasn't bleeding I was bruising when I was beautiful I learned how to suck in my stomach until it was nothing but ribs I learned how to drink only water mixed with vinegar but wasn't interested instead I gorged on sugar and let girls fuck me in the ass once I only wore red once a girl said I was so beautiful it made her ill and I kissed her and left wounded rouge on her mouth and her mother took my picture and once I learned how to get on my knees I very rarely got back up

The brief life of a stone figure

I met F and A and we ate oysters and compared the pumice of our bones.
In different cities I've become a blood myth. I've opened my legs like a pub door.
I've had a mouth gone funeral casket. At fourteen I didn't say no, I turned my
body into a girl hole. I fell in love with a drug girl she always had little roach burns
on her hands. I fell in love with F and F didn't care and we went to the park and
she fed me slate shards and we drank wine and mixed it with Zyrtec
because the thing about stone is that it's always allergic. F says, *one
day you'll open your legs for a stranger again but find nothing but marble slits/one
day you'll be a virgin again your hymen will be granite* so I tell her the closest I
came to being a virgin was when I took a girl in my mouth after service.

The death of S, Aphrodite & the kneeling basilisk

(in the voice of)

In the fall we are little gods/we drink only vodka/we try out prescription meds/
we learn how to enact the feminine neuroses assigned to us by men/we meet B
and F and they show us how to drink from broken bottles and how to eat butter
off the stick/F says she knows how to suck until there's nothing left of her/B has a
scar shaped like a cross on her stomach/they burn sage and money/in the Met we
find pictures of the kneeling women we find F and her stone cunt-womb her false
children/B says, *once I died/I already know what it is to have blood in my mouth
and nothing else*/F has an orchid she grew in rubble/we're nothing but cold marble
and girl

The carving of S/Aphrodite & F

Their bodies dust-mouths:
ancient carvers would penetrate
the figurines of female deities with sticks
to indicate penetrability/vulnerability
gouge their arms open with metal
put pins inside their cunts
the mounds of pubic bone a small earth
the nails carved into their bodies dust wounds
small bloody exit holes

Marble female figure

*"The recognition of distinct artistic personalities in Cycladic sculpture is
based upon recurring systems of proportion and details of execution. The
stylization of the human body that is elegant almost to the point of mannerism
is characteristic of the Bastis Master."*

covered my cuts with cornstarch mixed with boiling water
when we break it is only for the rain
I drove with a girl at night & let her finger me on an interstate
when I was a horse girl I always had dirt in my mouth & grass
stuck between my teeth
I let my hipbones turn into ravines so I learned how to break
before I got broken, learned how to swallow the earth until it spits back

The pathos of fertility, 1921, Germany

"Watercolor and transferred printing ink on paper, bordered with ink,
mounted on the verso of a lithograph by Paul Rohrbach"

Men say I'm a hysteric so I fuck their sisters.
Every time a man says bitch I swallow some girl's cum.
Every time I bleed I dig the clots out, let the red cake under my nails.
Men make a mythos out of female pain so I dismiss them.
I dismiss them until I get tired from it. I bleed
until I can't walk. I take fists into my cunt like some girls
learn to sing. A hysteric is a girl who can't be
disappeared, so I invent pathos for myself like shiny
new wounds. Fertility is only something invented
by men with nothing better to do.

Standing female figure wearing a strap & a necklace

"This sculpture is one of a group of statues associated with the South Arabian Bronze Age. It comes at the beginning of a figural tradition characterized by extreme simplification and symbolic strength. Represented is a standing female with a role of fat and deep groove emphasizing the belly and a clearly indicated pubic triangle. Her massive body is contained within a quadrangular space. The legs look truncated but the toes, like the hands and fingers, are indicated by incisions. She wears a strap across her body and a necklace. Subject and style invite comparison with Near Eastern and Aegean Neolithic statuary and with much later South Arabian statuary of the second century B.C. In early Anatolia and Greece—as in late Paleolithic Europe—nude females were dynamic, with curved, exaggeraged breasts, belly, and buttocks. By contrast, the frontal, profile, and back planes of the South Arabian sculpture are separated, emphasizing abstraction and containment within a blocklike form—features that characterize figural art of the region more than two thousand years later. Other similar statues were found near western highland settlements and the inner Hadramawt area. A few males appear ithyphallic, suggesting that these human or divine images were used in fertility rituals."

Dear F

The moon is a cunt. I've learned how to navigate the creeks at night, how to be bitten by something both alive and not. How to pretend a body is made out of stone until you are allowed to crumble. If you don't breathe you're not alive. When you bleed pretend it is sugar and always suck your red off of someone else's hands so they won't have to do it for you. These days, I am learning how to disappear, have taken up knives as a recreation. These days, I've forgotten that I have a mouth.

Figure of fertility goddess (2700 B.C.)

No information, Terracota, 2700-3000 B.C.

I swallowed three stones so that I would be fertile
I ate mud because they told me that to be pure is to be dirt

before I turned into a girl gone bone I broke my wrists,
spent a winter in casts, spent the whole time reapplying
lipstick until my mouth was a wound ready to get fucked
because really all anyone wants is blood on a dead girl's lips,
the metallic taste of after-death: like he said,
there's nothing more lovely than a pretty girl dying,
than tasting bullet grease between thighs, small eyes
and hands held up but not in prayer, terracotta lips:
when you wash away all that will be left is dried blood and talc

*I turned my legs into an open casket service/I gave myself an autopsy/I became a part
of the ground: always underneath someone*

when my wrists heal I carry my hands at a tilt for months,
spend every raining day inside waiting for my body to turn back to dirt

Figure of fertility goddess (2000 B.C.)

Dear F

Once a girl wanted me to act like a broken bird when she fucked me.
Slowly I am forgetting, slowly I am beginning to eat only sugar.
One of these days I will be resplendent, one of these days I will be freed.

I covered my skin in sequins to hide the bruises, I smeared silver under
my eyes to seem expensive, I had hate sex, my teeth bared the whole
time, kids used to throw dollars and pencils at me so I'd bend over, used
to watch me try to eat until eventually my jaw closed up and my ribs got
firefly-like. Once I stepped on glass just to see if it would cut.

Plaque with nude female in a shrine niche

"Limestone or terracotta plaques showing nude women in the niche of an Egyptian-form shrine were popular from 600-275 BC. Sometimes architectural pediments are carved and Bes figures or Hathor columns may be represented beside the niche; here traces of paint on the jambs can no longer be resolved into any particular form. The bobbed-haired voluptuous woman has a long history in the first millennium, but no precise identity. Small plaques like these are probably to be associated with the informal artworks distributed in conjunction with festivals celebrating a divine birth and fertility."

There's nothing better than seeing a slut tamed/once a girl fucked me so
she could tell her friends she did/a girl had a cocktail party story about
me and it went:

a girl is no longer a girl once she starts bleeding
but now I can't stop, am always gaping red
onto someone else's bedsheets
and crying to myself every time there's a full moon

Terracotta statuette of a nude woman

"This statuette likely represents the goddess Aphrodite."

what's it like to love a dead girl?

A. cold stars, the gasoline from an old factory, a man who doesn't understand "no," a girl with honey caking her teeth like fool's gold

B. a park at three in the morning and three bullet shots, a girl who once was named *L*, an empty car, the scar on your thigh, the scar on your back, the broken wishbone she made you, three black dots she stabbed into her arm with your ballpoint pen

C. chewing up irises on her bed because she told you to pretend to be feral again, like you were at 13, getting bullwhipped on her lap until your skin was an animal hide and you too were dead

Head of a woman, 220 B.C.

(Fertility, speaking as a 14-year-old girl)

Sunday like a stretch of dawn you found,
held it small and glistening
like a slash of something not us
in the dried up bed—
we were the moths and our wings
were that sort of blue-green bruise
and the red was still staining us
like the dark wet clay we found
underneath the pier, the sick damp
feeling spreading into our mouths
like the honey our priests used
to anoint us with before we
became unholy girls, that silence
like the still uterine quiet of baptism,
back when we could still be saved,
when your mouth was still a mouth
we would get sick off sugar packets
and let the grains dissolve into illness on our tongues—
this was before the midnight telephone hooks,
the house gone small with your withering.
Feral cats started circling our back doors, trying to sneak in
so we newspapered the windows to keep something
we didn't know out, your bandages like small
butterfly wings in the dark. This was before I met a girl
in a car at night and her car was filled with sugar wrappers—
old dried up candies glinting like minnows in the dark
ocean of her backseat. After, we walked through a cornfield
and she said *I just wanted to be holy/I didn't want to be*
this way/wrong, she wrote each psalm on her thigh with Sharpie:
An abomination/thou shall not lay shall not lay with your same,
the slick of the cornfield's skeins crunching under
our feet like small bodies. I etched her name

into my arm with her keys and pretended I didn't.
After you left, I stopped eating sugar and started drinking
salt mixed with tepid water, filled the house
with old stale pastries and let the frosting rot and mold.

Kneeling female deity

why are men so preoccupied with kneeling/
I long ago learned how to bend over/how to
prelude the injury by causing it before it can happen/
when girls call me slut I just suck the cunt out of their fingers
until my teeth ache blue from it

The history of bones

If another girl is killed if we find more bird skeletons in the yard if I dream of guns again if I once again spend the night on the floor if we again eat dirt if I again am bloodied if I bleed again if we no longer wear red if there's another girl who's been turned into nothing but gravestone

The history of violence

Once a girl ripped my skin, I have a teeth scar, I have so many letters I've been meaning to burn, I am so tired of night and wood floors and girls who think I'm more stone than flesh.

Self-biography as a hole

When they started calling me a hole I started contemplating A and F,
being a girl is like being viewed as nothing but chasm/once I bent down in a
Nordstrom's to strap her shoes and a girl tried to finger me like an absent hole
and kept trying even after I stood back up/sometimes I wonder what it would be
like to be filled completely: as in to have a body that cannot be entered anymore,
to be spaceless and nothing but unfuckable rock/once a girl told me to call her
Jesus/once I put a hand to my thigh and it came away covered in blood/
everyone knows that blood is sex so why am I always covered in it? Why did that
girl say my mouth was a wound? Why did she hook her fingers inside my lip/and
pull until the seam split like God?

Self-biography as a Venus

(in the voice of the Marble Venus)

This stone/this mouth/I am nothing but pumice and tears/I have a death wish/I could give birth like it's nothing but crying/I could swallow the ocean's salt/my body is Baltic amber/I am in stasis/I pray to no one/I once was slipped inside mouths to assist impregnation but I am infertile/every child I birth is nothing but air and invisible bones

Self-biography as a false saint

Dear Catherine

I know why you swallowed only cancer pus why you whipped your skin until all
that was left of your ribcage was muscle and bone.

Once I saw Jesus.
She was a blood mouth.

Once I hit my head on concrete and saw saints, oranges, dizzy blood.
My skull almost split like a cleaved fruit.
To be taken seriously a woman has to become nothing but a wound.

Once I wanted to be fleshless, like a hawk: nothing but bones and wings.

When you stopped menstruating they called you an angel.

Oh Catherine: don't you know blood and bones are the only holy things left?

Don't you know your ribcage is a false prayer?

Self-biography as a pregnant woman

> To get pregnant a woman must insert a halved date soaked in rosewater into her orifices and leave it in for twenty nights then eat it. She may not bleed. The date will become pure salt.
> —a medieval spell for infertility, B.C.

Dear F .

if I had a daughter I would drink only peppermint oil/if I could I would mother your stone/if I gave birth it would only be to blood/once I tried to plant flowers/once I tried to grow things/but then just cut all my hair off and wore only black silk/learned how to open my mouth so wide it becomes nothing/learned how to pray

Dear F

If I could I would eat you alive.
Whenever I break eggs they come out bloody.
If I could I would suck the pulp out of lemons until I became all salt.

Self-biography as a girl with no mouth

Let me be pure/let me be holeless
The safest girls are those who stay quiet
Saints would stitch their lips shut with black wire
I always said that one day I would be holy
I always said that one day I would be a swan
Mute and nothing but tar and lovely feathers
We used to mix vinegar with salt water
Gargle it to look for cuts inside our throats
I used to swab my own throat until I choked on the cotton
Once I coughed for so long my lungs fell out
Once I forgot how to speak
Once I became all stone
Once I was something not girl
Once I was a bird

Autobiography of a Venus figure

I was a bimbo and I had a following. When I cut my hair off men cried.
When I went into fields it was never alone. Bathrooms were my mecca. I
could drink until my throat gave out. I could eat cunt until exhausted.
Blood didn't faze me. I could slash myself open and still make it to dinner.
I could swallow until there was nothing left. I was beautiful in the autumn. I
owned leather. I kept handcuffs on one wrist always. I was mostly scar
tissue and broken glass.

Autobiography of something fertile

Being impregnateable is exhausting. I want to menstruate until I'm nothing, I want a body gone stone, to be something dried up and washed up on a shore. I want a hole that can't be entered: I want to be all orifice and no consequence.

Autobiography of basalt & broken stones

Fossil is my new name, soon my bones will be twigs and I will be no longer beautiful. Everyone loves the idea of a woman gone sand. One day I will become plant entirely. One day I will swallow the sun and become something more than a stone girl.

Autobiography of a wound

Dear F

The first time I died I was seven. Every girl has a suicide story. It's like stars falling, something we pretend is rare. My bones are really small buildings. My mouth holds multitudes. Sometimes I pretend to be dumb to see how dead they think I am. I have more scars than basalt. My marrow is really sea salt. One day I will open my eyes and find nothing. One day I will learn to love. One day we will be whole, one day we will open our mouths to the sky and swallow.

NOTES AND ACKNOWLEDGMENTS

Variations of "*Head of a woman, 220 B.C.,*" "*Self-portrait as a drowning city,*" and "*Figure of Isis-Aphrodite*" have appeared in *Poetry Crush* and *Rookie*. Variations of "*Self-biography as a girl with no mouth,*" "*Self-portrait as a wound, a bird skull, & a stone,*" and "*Self-portrait as the lake in which they were drowned*" have appeared in the *American Poetry Review*. The titles and opening quotes to the fertility poems are taken from The Met's online collection of fertility figurines.